Prayers for Mental Renewal

H.B Sky

Published by H.B Sky, 2025.

PRAYERS FOR MENTAL RENEWAL

First edition. November 22, 2025.

ISBN: 979-8232853372

Written by H.B Sky.

Table of Contents

To every weary mind and burdened heart

may these prayers offer a starting place

where your strength returns slowly

and peace begins its gentle work.

To those rebuilding their inner worlds,

learning to trust God again,

with the parts of themselves

they barely understand

this book is for you.

"But the fruit of the Spirit is love, joy, peace, forbearance, kindness, goodness, faithfulness, gentleness and self-control."
— Galatians 5:22–23 (NIV)

PREFACE

The mind is a landscape.

Constantly evolving — changing, growing, stretching, and sometimes struggling beneath pressures seen and unseen.

I wrote this book for the moments when life feels heavy, when clarity slips away, and when the soul longs for rest but cannot quite reach it.

Prayers for Mental Renewal is a companion for the uncertain hours: a collection of gentle reflections and heartfelt petitions shaped around the Fruit of the Spirit. Each section offers a simple truth, a moment of grounding, and a prayer you can return to again and again.

My hope is that this book becomes a place of refuge, not because it solves every tension, but because it guides you back to the One who restores the mind, calms the heart, and illuminates understanding. These words are meant to slow the racing thoughts, soften the inner noise, and remind you that renewal is not an event but a steady return to God's presence.

Take your time with these prayers.

Reflect. Let God meet you where you are.

May each page help you rediscover clarity, resilience, and spiritual calm.

INTRODUCTION

"But the fruit of the Spirit is love, joy, peace, forbearance, kindness, goodness, faithfulness, gentleness and self-control." — Galatians 5:22–23 (NIV)

The Fruit of the Holy Spirit has always fascinated me, not as a list of virtues to achieve but as evidence of God's work within us. Love, joy, peace, patience, kindness, goodness, faithfulness, gentleness, and self-control are not traits we grow by willpower alone. They are the natural outflow of a heart that remains connected to God, even in seasons when the mind feels overwhelmed or weary.

This book was born from the realization that many of us long for mental renewal, yet often overlook the spiritual nourishment that makes that renewal possible. The Fruit of the Spirit is God's way of restoring us from the inside out. Each fruit holds a specific kind of healing:

love steadies us,
joy lifts us,
peace grounds us,
forbearance calms us,
kindness softens us,
goodness strengthens us,
faithfulness anchors us,
gentleness settles us,
and self-control directs us.

In these pages, you will find prayers shaped by each of these fruits. My intention is to invite you into a deeper experience of God's transformative presence. These prayers are not meant to pressure you into becoming more; they are meant to draw you into resting in the One who already sustains you.

As you read, may the Holy Spirit water the places within you that have grown dry. May you feel each fruit take root, flourish, and renew your mind with strength, clarity, and peace.

LOVE

Where there is love, the soul gains room to move.

~

God,
refresh our minds and hearts,
clearing clutter and confusion.
Let thoughts flow freely without weight,
giving space for insight and calm.
Teach us to release tension,
replacing worry with clarity and focus.
Inspire creative solutions
and hopeful perspectives in our daily choices.
Guide our reflections
so they cultivate strength and serenity,
allowing mental energy to rebuild with purpose.
Help us embrace new ideas with courage,
leaving behind patterns that hinder growth.
May each breath renew our spirit,
shaping resilience,
calm,
and understanding.
Let the light of love restore our inner landscape.
Amen

Love shapes how we use our time.

~

God,
guide our attention to what truly matters,
allowing wisdom to direct our time.
Clear distractions that fragment the mind
and exhaust the spirit.
Teach us to prioritize activities
that nourish thought and focus.
Help us find rhythm in our work,
resting when needed,
acting with precision when called.
Let love-infused intention structure our days,
creating harmony and energy.
Inspire us to approach tasks with clarity and calm,
using mental strength efficiently.
May our minds remain flexible yet grounded,
capable of responding with creativity and insight.
Amen

A life steered by love holds steady through change.

~

God,
steady our thoughts in seasons of change,
restoring balance when uncertainty arises.
Teach us to see transitions
as opportunities to grow and adapt.
Help us to embrace new circumstances
without fear,
trusting insight gained through reflection.
Inspire us to release rigidity,
letting love guide decisions
with steadiness and purpose.
Restore our mental energy,
replacing stress with resilience.
Let clarity shape our perspective,
allowing us to navigate challenges with poise.
May our minds remain anchored in understanding,
able to find calm amid turbulence.
Amen

Love strengthens a path more than force ever will.

~

God,
strengthen our mental resolve
with patience and care
rather than force.
Teach us to approach difficulties
with insight,
responding thoughtfully
rather than reacting impulsively.
Help us build internal structures
that support focus and perseverance.
Let love-infused reflection
replace strain and tension,
creating mental stability.
Inspire calm judgment,
reinforcing our ability to make wise,
measured choices.
May our minds grow in resilience and flexibility,
able to navigate complexity with clarity.
Let mental renewal guide our paths
and fortify our inner life.
Amen

Some days rely on love the way roots rely on rain.

~

God,
nourish our minds like rain feeds roots,
replenishing what has been exhausted.
Clear mental fatigue,
allowing clarity and creativity to flourish.
Help us invest energy
where it produces growth and insight.
Inspire reflection that strengthens focus
and illuminates understanding.
Teach us to rest when needed,
giving space for renewal without guilt.
Let love guide mental energy,
encouraging deep,
constructive thinking.
May our minds awaken with purpose
and adaptability,
open to learning and growth.
Restore the vigor
that allows thought to bloom
fully and calmly.
Amen

Love sharpens the spine of anyone who lives with purpose.

~

God,
grant us courage
to face mental challenges
with clarity and determination.
Let love reinforce focus,
strengthening commitment to meaningful work.
Teach us to release fear and distraction,
trusting insight and intention.
Inspire confidence
in our ability to persevere through difficulty,
keeping our minds anchored in calm resolve.
Help us balance reflection with action,
using energy wisely and purposefully.
May mental clarity illuminate each choice,
allowing thoughtful,
confident steps forward.
Restore vitality to tired thought
and illuminate understanding.
Let renewed focus
guide our paths toward growth.
Amen

Ideas grow stronger when love fuels the work.

~

God,
nurture creativity and insight,
letting inspiration flow without obstruction.
Guide our minds to explore new possibilities
while remaining grounded.
Teach us to see patterns and solutions
that were hidden by fatigue or doubt.
Inspire collaboration and learning,
allowing love to fuel understanding.
Restore mental clarity,
giving patience for process
and courage for experimentation.
Help us value reflection as much as action,
balancing thought and purpose.
May our minds regenerate daily,
becoming more resourceful,
flexible,
and insightful.
Let renewed thought
transform our efforts into lasting impact.
Amen

Love turns a single step into a direction worth keeping.

~

God,
guide each step with clarity,
turning small choices into meaningful direction.
Teach us to focus our mental energy
on what fosters growth and understanding.
Inspire patience in decision-making,
letting insight replace haste.
Help us release mental clutter
that distracts from purpose and vision.
Restore perspective and flexibility,
allowing us to adapt without losing composure.
Let renewed thought illuminate paths,
turning uncertainty into opportunity.
May our minds maintain steady focus,
guided by love and wisdom.
Amen

Every hard edge softens when love governs the response.

~

God,
soften mental tension,
allowing understanding
and empathy to shape responses.
Teach us to approach challenges with composure,
turning frustration into insight.
Inspire thoughtful reflection
that calms reactive impulses.
Help us replace sharp judgment
with measured discernment,
letting love guide perspective.
Restore balance
when thoughts feel rigid or strained.
Let clarity and calm flow freely,
strengthening resilience and adaptability.
May our minds remain open yet anchored,
able to respond with insight
rather than stress.
Amen

A mind guided by love doesn't shrink under pressure.

~

God,
fortify our minds under pressure,
letting care guide every thought.
Teach us to face challenges
with clear judgment and steady focus.
Restore confidence and reduce doubt,
giving mental resilience the space to grow.
Inspire creative solutions
and measured responses to complex situations.
Help us release tension that clouds insight
or restricts perspective.
Let renewed mental energy cultivate wisdom,
patience,
and decisive action.
May our thoughts remain balanced,
flexible,
and guided by compassion.
Amen

Love can hold people together without binding them.

~

God,
help us maintain mental freedom
in relationships,
supporting others
without overextending control.
Teach our minds to balance connection
with discernment,
letting empathy guide understanding.
Inspire flexibility and openness,
fostering insight without attachment or pressure.
Restore perspective,
allowing love to shape clarity and focus.
Help us release mental patterns
that bind unnecessarily,
promoting calm and resilience.
Let thoughtful reflection guide decisions,
encouraging wisdom
and renewal in every interaction.
May our minds remain adaptive,
compassionate,
and clear.
Amen

Fact and faith wrestle often, but love steadies the outcome.

~

God,
steady our thinking
when doubt and tension arise.
Let insight guide choices
amid uncertainty,
reinforcing perspective with care.
Teach us to reconcile competing priorities
with understanding,
using reflection to find calm.
Restore clarity to fatigued thought,
encouraging discernment in action.
Inspire patience,
balance,
and inner focus,
even when circumstances challenge
peace of mind.
Help mental renewal take root,
enabling resilience,
creativity,
and effective decision-making.
May clarity guide every step
and every interaction,
strengthening insight and calm.
Amen

Communities rise when love sets the rhythm of their choices.

~

God,
guide communities and minds alike
toward harmony and shared purpose.
Inspire collective thought
that values clarity,
reflection,
and care.
Teach us to shape environments
that support learning,
creativity,
and mental restoration.
Restore insight where distraction
or tension prevails.
Help us invest energy in actions
that foster growth,
understanding,
and renewal.
Let thoughtfulness define interactions,
promoting wisdom
and constructive action.
May renewed mental focus create stability,
collaboration,
and lasting progress,
guided by love and intention.
Amen

Love gives a task more weight than fear ever could.

~

God,
grant us courage
to approach tasks with clarity and purpose.
Replace fear and distraction
with focus and determination.
Teach us to channel mental energy
toward constructive and meaningful action.
Inspire insight that transforms routine effort
into growth and accomplishment.
Help us navigate challenges calmly,
letting renewed thought
guide decisions and shape results.
Restore mental vitality and patience,
allowing resilience
and creativity to flourish.
May every task
be an opportunity for reflection,
understanding,
and renewal,
strengthening both mind and spirit.
Amen

Even in chaos, love marks the path that leads forward.

~

God,
illuminate the path through chaos,
letting mental clarity guide every step.
Teach us to release confusion
and maintain perspective,
even when circumstances are unpredictable.
Restore focus and insight,
allowing thoughtful action
to replace reactive decision-making.
Inspire patience and discernment,
letting love shape responses and priorities.
Help us maintain calm awareness,
recognizing opportunity amid disorder.
May mental renewal bring direction,
resilience,
and understanding,
keeping each choice purposeful and steady.
Let renewed thought lead the way forward
with confidence and balance.
Amen

JOY

When the mind finds joy, possibility widens.

~

God,
let our minds discover joy
that widens perception and possibility.
Clear mental blocks
and awaken creativity where routine dulls insight.
Teach us to notice small sparks of happiness
that expand thinking and lift spirits.
Restore energy to thoughts
that stagnate under fatigue or worry.
Help us embrace curiosity and optimism,
allowing mental clarity to flourish.
Inspire reflection that opens doors
previously unseen,
shaping understanding
with lightness and ease.
May joy become a catalyst for renewed focus,
adaptability,
and wisdom in every choice.
Amen

A task built with joy holds its shape longer.

~

God,
infuse our work with joy,
letting effort take shape and endure.
Guide our minds to focus on purpose
rather than pressure,
sustaining energy through thoughtful intention.
Teach us to celebrate progress,
however small,
knowing it strengthens momentum and clarity.
Restore enthusiasm
where doubt or fatigue clouds thinking.
Inspire patience and insight,
allowing tasks to develop naturally and fully.
Help us find rhythm and ease,
letting joy anchor persistence and resilience.
May mental renewal flow through each action,
producing thoughtful outcomes and lasting strength.
Amen

Some paths open only after joy enters the room.

~

God,
open our paths as joy enters,
revealing opportunities unseen before.
Clear hesitation
and hesitation-born fear from our minds.
Teach us to approach life with openness,
letting mental energy expand into new directions.
Restore confidence and flexibility,
allowing insight to guide choices with ease.
Inspire reflection that uncovers possibilities
and strengthens understanding.
Help us embrace creativity,
innovation,
and clarity in decision-making.
May joy illuminate
mental paths that were blocked,
fostering calm,
focus,
and renewed vision in every step.
Amen

Ideas stretch farther when joy supports them.

~

God,
support our ideas with joy,
letting imagination stretch beyond limitations.
Teach our minds to nurture creativity
without fear or constraint.
Restore mental energy
where doubt or fatigue weakens clarity.
Inspire insight that combines discipline with delight,
producing results that endure.
Help us approach challenges with optimism
and adaptability,
letting joy guide perspective.
May every thought become a seed of growth,
every reflection a source of renewed energy
and understanding.
Let the mind thrive in exploration,
innovation,
and ease.
Amen

Even small efforts gain force once joy joins in.

~

God,
let joy enter our small efforts,
giving them force and direction.
Guide our minds to see value in every step,
no matter how modest.
Teach us to embrace persistence with lightness,
freeing thought from unnecessary strain.
Restore clarity and focus,
allowing mental energy to flow efficiently.
Inspire creative approaches to challenges,
seeing opportunities where others see obstacles.
Help us approach work with calm confidence,
letting joy amplify results.
May mental renewal arise from enthusiasm,
patience,
and reflection in all tasks.
Amen

A person carrying joy walks with steadier aim.

~

God,
help us carry joy within,
walking with steadier aim through uncertainty.
Clear confusion and distraction,
letting intention and clarity guide thought.
Teach us to approach challenges
with focus tempered by delight.
Restore mental resilience where fatigue
or doubt dull perception.
Inspire reflection and adaptability,
allowing insight to shape understanding and direction.
Help us act with confidence,
even in complex or shifting circumstances.
May joy strengthen focus,
sharpen intention,
and renew mental energy
with each thoughtful step we take.
Amen

The future feels less rigid when joy influences the next choice.

~

God,
soften rigidity in our view of the future,
letting joy influence choices with ease.
Teach our minds to imagine possibilities
beyond limits or fear.
Restore flexibility and vision
where uncertainty creates hesitation.
Inspire confidence and optimism
in decision-making,
letting joy guide perspective.
Help us release fixation on obstacles
and embrace paths of innovation.
May mental renewal flourish as hope
and enthusiasm shape each plan.
Let every choice be informed by clarity,
delight,
and adaptability,
producing thoughtful,
resilient outcomes.
Amen

Progress sharpens when joy guides the momentum.

~

God,
sharpen progress
by letting joy guide momentum,
balancing effort with ease.
Teach our minds to approach tasks
with insight and resilience,
letting enthusiasm fuel persistence.
Restore focus and clarity
when mental strain or fatigue
threatens forward movement.
Inspire innovative thinking
and strategic reflection,
allowing energy to flow efficiently.
Help us recognize patterns of success
and adapt approaches with creativity.
May renewed mental focus
transform effort into growth,
sustaining both clarity and satisfaction.
Let joy strengthen every step and intention.
Amen

A conversation shaped by joy can shift an entire day.

~

God,
shape our conversations with joy,
allowing them to influence entire days.
Teach our minds to speak
with insight and receptivity,
fostering understanding and connection.
Restore patience and clarity
where tension or miscommunication arises.
Inspire openness to new perspectives,
letting joy guide interaction and thought.
Help us listen deeply,
respond thoughtfully,
and reflect with composure.
May mental renewal flourish
as dialogue strengthens perception,
empathy,
and adaptability.
Let every word carry intention,
lightness,
and insight.
Amen

Direction becomes easier to claim when joy stays in the mix.

~

God,
let direction become easier to claim
when joy informs decisions.
Clear uncertainty and hesitation
from our minds.
Teach us to focus on possibilities
rather than obstacles.
Restore clarity and balance,
letting mental energy flow toward meaningful outcomes.
Inspire reflective thinking
that recognizes opportunity and potential.
Help us act decisively and calmly,
guided by insight and optimism.
May mental renewal flourish as joy shapes perspective,
strengthens resolve,
and fosters thoughtful adaptability.
Let every choice
be informed by confidence and ease.
Amen

A mind infused with joy adapts in ways fear never manages.

~

God,
infuse our minds with joy,
enabling adaptability beyond fear's reach.
Teach us to approach change
and challenge with curiosity
rather than resistance.
Restore flexibility and insight
where stress or rigidity constricts thought.
Inspire reflection that transforms uncertainty
into opportunity and innovation.
Help us act with calm courage,
letting mental clarity lead decisions.
May joy cultivate resilience,
adaptability,
and focus,
strengthening the mind's ability to navigate complexity.
Let renewed thinking flourish,
guided by optimism
and thoughtful energy in every choice we make.
Amen

Work rooted in joy develops a different kind of strength.

~

God,
root our work in joy,
letting effort develop enduring strength.
Teach our minds to focus on purpose
and fulfillment,
balancing challenge with delight.
Restore persistence where fatigue
or doubt diminishes energy.
Inspire creativity,
patience,
and insight,
allowing tasks to mature fully.
Help us recognize the transformative power
of joy in shaping results and perspective.
May mental renewal grow from engagement,
reflection,
and lightness in action.
Let each effort carry energy and resilience.
Amen

Some breakthroughs depend on joy to break the stale patterns.

~

God,
let joy spark breakthroughs
that dissolve stale thinking.
Teach our minds
to embrace new angles and possibilities.
Restore flexibility where routine
or rigidity blocks insight.
Inspire innovative reflection
that illuminates pathways and opportunities.
Help us approach challenges with curiosity,
optimism,
and clarity.
May mental renewal take root,
allowing insight,
adaptability,
and energy to flourish.
Let every breakthrough remind us
that joy reshapes perspective,
energizes thought,
and opens the mind to discovery.
Amen

A plan gains new angles when joy turns the wheel.

~

God,
turn the wheel of our plans with joy,
revealing new angles and possibilities.
Teach our minds
to see beyond habit or expectation.
Restore perspective where rigidity
or fatigue narrows thought.
Inspire flexibility,
insight,
and careful reflection,
allowing mental energy to flow freely.
Help us adapt with ease,
finding opportunity in change and challenge.
May mental renewal flourish
as joy informs every decision,
guiding perspective and resilience.
Let plans,
actions,
and ideas carry insight,
purpose,
and flexibility through every thoughtful step.
Amen

Even in a demanding moment, joy can enter like a spark and change the rhythm.

~

God,
let joy enter demanding moments,
changing rhythm and perspective.
Teach our minds to respond with calm,
even under pressure.
Restore patience and insight where stress
or fatigue clouds thought.
Inspire creativity,
adaptability,
and thoughtful action in every circumstance.
Help us embrace challenges
with lightness and optimism,
letting joy influence pace and decisions.
May mental renewal flow freely,
transforming strain into insight,
energy,
and resilience.
Let every moment carry the spark of focus and joy,
guiding thought and action alike.
Amen

PEACE

Peace isn't a place to arrive at, but a choice to practice.

~

God,
guide us to practice peace deliberately,
even when circumstances feel chaotic.
Teach our minds to pause,
breathe,
and reset thought,
restoring calm and balance.
Help us release judgment,
letting compassion and understanding shape perspective.
Inspire patience and insight that steady the mind,
even amid tension.
Restore clarity where conflict
or worry clouds focus.
May inner tranquility root deeply,
radiating outward to interactions
and decisions,
fostering renewal in thought and spirit.
Let every choice reflect calm,
wisdom,
and intentional ease.
Amen

Even the smallest reset can restore a sense of peace.

~

God,
help us find stillness
in the smallest ways we find rest,
letting these brief moments
restore clarity and perspective.
Teach our minds to seek calm
amidst busyness,
valuing reflection over haste.
Restore insight and balance
where mental strain accumulates.
Inspire gentle thought
that nurtures calm and focus.
Help us approach challenges with composure,
letting reflection guide decisions.
May mental renewal grow through consistent,
intentional pauses,
shaping resilience,
focus,
and inner ease.
Let peace guide our minds and actions,
renewing strength
with each thoughtful breath.
Amen

Peace grows when judgment falls away.

~

God,
remove harsh judgment from our thinking,
allowing acceptance and understanding
to guide mental clarity.
Teach our minds to release criticism,
cultivating insight and adaptability.
Restore calm
where conflict or negativity clouds perception.
Inspire reflective thought
that values perspective and empathy.
Help us nurture environments
where peace flourishes,
shaping interactions and decisions.
May mental renewal
grow through openness and discernment,
fostering focus,
resilience,
and harmony in every situation.
Let calm shape thought,
bringing clarity
and strength to mind and spirit alike.
Amen

A steady mind carries peace like a hidden treasure.

~

God,
help our minds carry peace as a hidden treasure,
steady and quiet
even when life shifts unexpectedly.
Teach us to draw on inner stability,
using calm reflection to guide choices.
Restore focus and discernment
where stress or distraction threatens clarity.
Inspire insight and composure,
strengthening thought and decision-making.
Help us anchor renewal in calm,
letting steady perspective shape understanding and action.
May every day
include moments of mental grounding
that restore balance,
focus,
and thoughtful energy.
Let peace become a foundation for clarity and resilience.
Amen

Moments of silence can speak louder than words of conflict.

~

God,
let silence speak within our minds,
giving clarity where noise or conflict obscures thought.
Teach our minds to embrace reflection
as a source of insight and renewal.
Restore balance where tension or chaos overwhelms.
Inspire mental stillness that fosters understanding,
adaptability,
and composure.
Help us act thoughtfully,
guided by calm and clarity,
rather than reaction.
May inner peace shape perspective,
producing resilience,
focus,
and energy for meaningful action.
Let moments of silence renew thought and spirit,
guiding every decision with intention and ease.
Amen

Peace thrives where patience and understanding meet.

~

God,
help patience and understanding
nurture peace within us.
Teach our minds to listen deeply,
weigh options calmly,
and act with insight.
Restore clarity where frustration
or haste clouds judgment.
Inspire mental flexibility
that resolves tension and promotes focus.
Help us approach challenges
with empathy and wisdom,
letting inner calm guide reflection and choice.
May mental renewal grow
as patience shapes thought
and understanding strengthens perspective.
Let peace root deeply,
shaping action,
interaction,
and every mental process.
Amen

To nurture peace, start by easing the tension inside yourself.

~

God,
guide us to ease tension within,
cultivating peace at the center of thought.
Teach our minds to release pressure and control,
embracing clarity and adaptability.
Restore calm where anxiety
or fatigue disrupts focus.
Inspire reflection
that strengthens composure and insight.
Help us approach mental challenges with balance,
letting thoughtful decision-making
replace stress-driven reaction.
May inner renewal flourish
as peace anchors the mind,
allowing focus to grow steadily.
Let calm influence every thought,
shaping actions
and restoring energy for meaningful effort.
Amen

Peace is the calm current beneath the chaos of life.

~

God,
let peace flow beneath the turbulence of life,
grounding thought in composure.
Teach our minds to hold perspective
amid unpredictability.
Restore mental focus where stress
or pressure threatens composure.
Inspire reflection
that turns obstacles into lessons
and tension into insight.
Help us act from calm understanding
rather than reaction,
letting clarity guide decisions.
May mental renewal take root
through steady awareness,
resilience,
and discernment.
Let inner peace shape thinking,
providing calm strength for every task and interaction.
Amen

Choosing peace doesn't mean you're a shirker; it strengthens your path.

~

God,
show us that choosing peace strengthens our path
rather than weakens it.
Teach our minds to resist impulsive reaction
and embrace calm intention.
Restore focus where conflict
or agitation clouds judgment.
Inspire thoughtful reflection
that strengthens insight and steadies mental energy.
Help us act decisively with composure,
letting inner tranquility shape decisions.
May mental renewal grow as peace guides perception,
action,
and interaction,
producing clarity,
resilience,
and purposeful direction.
Let strength emerge from calm,
reinforcing every step we take in thought and life.
Amen

Peace comes when we let go of needing to control everything.

~

God,
help us release the need to control every outcome,
letting peace shape our responses.
Teach our minds to trust discernment
over compulsion,
releasing tension and cultivating calm.
Restore clarity where anxiety
or expectation distorts perspective.
Inspire insight
and reflection that strengthen
understanding and adaptability.
Help us approach mental challenges
with patience and composure,
allowing renewal to flourish.
May inner peace radiate outward,
influencing interactions,
decisions,
and thought patterns.
Let mental clarity and calm
become enduring companions,
shaping growth,
focus,
and resilience.
Amen

Inner peace radiates outward, shaping the world subtly.

~

God,
let inner peace radiate through our thoughts,
subtly shaping our engagement with the world.
Teach our minds to balance reflection with action,
calming reactionary impulses.
Restore focus and insight where tension
or fatigue clouds perception.
Inspire composure that strengthens adaptability,
patience,
and clarity.
Help us act with intention,
letting mental renewal flow from calm
and thoughtful presence.
May every interaction carry steadiness and clarity,
reinforcing mental energy and insight.
Let peace guide thought,
decision-making,
and understanding,
creating resilience
and harmony within and around us.
Amen

A heart open to compromise is fertile ground for peace.

~

God,
nurture a heart open to compromise,
allowing peace to grow in every choice.
Teach our minds to weigh perspectives
with clarity and understanding.
Restore calm where rigidity
or impatience obstructs thought.
Inspire reflection that cultivates insight,
empathy,
and flexibility.
Help us approach challenges
with balance and composure,
letting thoughtful decision-making guide action.
May mental renewal flourish
as openness shapes perception and strengthens focus.
Let inner peace become the foundation of clear,
resilient,
and adaptive thought,
fostering harmony and wisdom
in mind and spirit.
Amen

Peace is woven through small acts of kindness and respect.

~

God,
weave peace into
small acts of kindness and respect,
letting thoughtfulness
shape our mental energy.
Teach our minds to notice opportunities
to cultivate calm and understanding.
Restore clarity where impatience
or irritation arises.
Inspire reflection that strengthens insight,
composure,
and adaptability.
Help us approach life with quiet intention,
allowing small gestures to reinforce inner peace.
May mental renewal grow from consistent,
thoughtful choices that shape perspective,
behavior,
and understanding.
Let every action reflect calm,
nurturing the mind and spirit.
Amen

Even in storms, peace can exist like a strong anchor.

~

God,
anchor peace within our hearts
even in the midst of storms.
Teach our minds to hold steady,
finding calm amid chaos.
Restore clarity and focus
where tension or fear threatens composure.
Inspire reflection that transforms stress
into understanding and resilience.
Help us act with balance,
letting mental renewal
emerge from steady insight
and thoughtful attention.
May inner peace sustain perception,
decisions,
and actions,
creating clarity and strength
despite external turbulence.
Let tranquility
become a foundation for mental clarity.
Amen

The pursuit of peace begins with seeing value in every perspective.

~

God,
guide the pursuit of peace
by helping us see value
in every perspective.
Teach our minds to weigh differences
with curiosity and discernment.
Restore openness where rigidity
or bias limits understanding.
Inspire reflection that fosters empathy,
insight,
and calm.
Help us act thoughtfully,
letting mental renewal
take root in balanced perception
and measured choice.
May inner peace shape thinking,
decision-making,
and action,
cultivating clarity,
composure,
and resilience.
Let every perspective enrich thought,
creating harmony,
focus,
and renewed energy for mind and spirit.
Amen

FORBEARANCE

Forebearance turns friction into quiet understanding.

~

God,
guide us when friction rises,
shaping our reactions
so we aim for growth
instead of escalation.
Strengthen our resolve
to pause before speaking,
so our choices create progress
rather than barriers.
Help us use steady restraint
that protects relationships
and opens paths
toward better understanding.
Teach us to respond
with balanced judgment,
turning strain
into opportunities to cooperate.
Let our decisions reflect purpose
rooted in wisdom.
Shape our character
so we move past impulse
and choose responses
that support lasting stability,
dignity,
and shared direction.
Keep us grounded
as we build stronger bonds
through thoughtful action.
Amen

True strength often shows in the patience to wait without complaint.

~

God,
help us wait with strength
when circumstances slow our plans.
Build in us the resolve
to hold steady without complaint,
allowing our decisions to form
through maturity instead of impulse.
Teach us to trust
that time
often reveals what rushed choices conceal.
Guide our thoughts
so we act from grounded conviction
rather than frustration.
Strengthen our ability
to move through delay
with solid intention,
keeping our course aligned with long-term
outcomes rather than short-term emotion.
Support us in choosing actions that shape progress,
even when the path requires endurance
and measured response.
Lead us toward wiser futures.
Amen

Forebearance is a bridge built from restraint and insight.

~

God,
help us build responses rooted
in restraint supported by insight.
When tension rises,
remind us that steadiness can bridge conflict
more effectively than force.
Grant us the discipline
to speak only when it strengthens the moment,
not when it satisfies impulse.
Guide our steps
so we act in ways that protect dignity on all sides.
Teach us to recognize
that holding back at the right time
can move challenges toward solutions.
Shape our character
so our choices create stability
, cooperation,
and openings for better outcomes.
Let our restraint support genuine progress
that benefits everyone involved.
Amen

Enduring without resentment reveals the depth of character.

~

God,
help us endure difficulty
without allowing resentment
to shape our reactions.
Strengthen our resolve
to move through pressure
with balanced intent.
Remind us
that character grows most
when we respond with discipline
instead of bitterness.
Guide our decisions
so we release the urge to retaliate
and choose actions
that keep us aligned with integrity.
Teach us to turn strain into construction
rather than damage.
Let our endurance reveal depth
rather than exhaustion.
Protect our hearts from the traps of anger,
and lead us toward choices
that strengthen relationships,
expand growth,
and uphold dignity for all.
Amen

To exercise forebearance is to choose calm over reaction.

~

God,
guide us toward calm responses
when we face provocation.
Strengthen our ability
to pause before reacting,
allowing wisdom to take the lead
instead of raw emotion.
Teach us to choose a steady path
where our actions support solutions
rather than add fuel to conflict.
Help us use restraint as a tool
that shapes stronger connections
and healthier outcomes.
Remind us that we are not defined by impulse
but by the direction we choose.
Shape our thinking
so we prioritize peace with purpose,
building environments
where growth can take root.
Support us as we pursue better ways forward.
Amen

Quiet tolerance can shift storms into gentle currents.

~

God,
help us transform storms
into manageable currents
through deliberate restraint.
Strengthen our inner composure
so we respond with direction
rather than disruption.
Grant us the resolve to hold steady
even when circumstances press us toward reaction.
Shape our thoughts
so we seek solutions rather than victory.
Teach us to redirect tense moments
toward building rather than breaking.
Let our steadiness open space for cooperation
that once felt unreachable.
Guide us in shaping outcomes
that strengthen relationships
and create new possibilities.
Help us carry this approach into every challenge,
turning turmoil into opportunities for progress.
Amen

Forebearance is itself controlled power.

~

God,
remind us that restraint
is strength used with purpose.
Help us wield our power
through measured responses
instead of unchecked impulse.
Teach us to recognizethat true capability
shows when we choose direction over reaction.
Strengthen our resolve to act with intention,
shaping environments
that allow understanding and growth.
Guide our thinking
so we avoid actions that fracture connection.
Help us use our influence constructively,
creating outcomes rooted in stability
rather than turmoil.
Let our decisions reflect depth
shaped through discipline,
revealing strength
that supports progress for everyone involved.
Lead us into futures built with wisdom.
Amen

Even in provocation, forebearance preserves dignity.

~

God,
guide us when provoked,
helping us hold to dignity
rather than surrender to reaction.
Strengthen our resolve
so we do not let others determine our direction.
Teach us to safeguard our inner balance,
responding with grounded purpose
that protects relationships.
Remind us that calm decisions
often repair what anger breaks.
Support us in choosing responses
that uphold who we strive to be,
not who frustration urges us to become.
Let our restraint demonstrate honor and stability.
Help us stand firm in our values,
shaping moments of tension into opportunities
for better understanding and cooperation.
Amen

Time often rewards those who practice thoughtful restraint.

~

God,
help us trust the slow rewards
that come from steady patience.
Strengthen us to wait with direction,
allowing time to reveal paths we could not see in haste.
Teach us to hold steady long enough
for wisdom to surface.
Guide our steps so we do not rush into choices
that weaken our future.
Remind us that progress formed through discipline
often lasts longer than quick fixes shaped by impulse.
Let our actions reflect conviction
built through thoughtful timing.
Walk with us as we cultivate endurance
that shapes stronger outcomes
and more grounded decisions.
Amen

Forebearance softens conflict without losing clarity.

~

God,
help us use patience to soften conflict
without losing our sense of purpose.
Strengthen our ability to respond with steadiness
that redirects tension toward improvement.
Teach us to separate urgency from impulse
so our actions serve progress rather than reaction.
Guide our thoughts to remain open
even in heated moments.
Let our calm decisions create conditions
where solutions can form.
Remind us that strength lies not in force
but in disciplined choice.
Support us as we shape interactions
that encourage cooperation,
clarity of direction,
and renewed trust among all involved.
Lead us toward constructive resolution.
Amen

The most potent responses are shaped by forebearance, not impulse.

~

God,
guide us to respond with measured strength
rather than impulse.
Help us recognize that the strongest path
often forms through patience shaped with intention.
Teach us to pause long enough
to choose words that build,
not break.
Strengthen our resolve so we refuse
to let frustration control our actions.
Let our responses carry purpose rooted in wisdom,
creating outcomes that uplift everyone involved.
Support us in shaping interactions
that reflect our deepest values.
Lead us to move through conflict
with grounded confidence,
transforming pressure into a chance
for better understanding and shared progress.
Amen

Tolerating imperfection teaches resilience in both self and others.

~

God,
teach us to accept imperfection in ourselves
and others so we grow in resilience.
Strengthen our willingness
to hold steady when flaws surface,
allowing us to learn instead of blame.
Guide us to respond with perspective
that sees beyond the moment.
Help us recognize that every challenge
offers material for development.
Let our restraint prevent unnecessary conflict
and give space for growth.
Shape our mindset so we seek improvement,
not unrealistic control.
Support us as we build relationships that mature
through understanding and perseverance.
Lead us into stronger unity
shaped through balanced expectation
and steady resolve.
Amen

Forebearance turns challenges into lessons rather than battles.

~

God,
help us transform challenges into lessons
rather than battles.
Strengthen our resolve to step back before reacting,
allowing us to see what the moment can teach.
Guide us to respond with purpose
that moves situations forward.
Teach us to value growth over victory.
Let our choices reflect commitment
to becoming wiser through every test.
Support us as we navigate tension
without fueling it.
Shape our thinking so we meet difficulty
with intention that builds deeper understanding.
Lead us toward outcomes
that expand cooperation,
maturity,
and renewed strength
within our relationships and communities.
Amen

Holding back in kindness often builds deeper trust than speaking out.

~

God,
help us hold back our words
when speaking would hinder progress.
Strengthen our ability to pause out of kindness,
allowing room for better outcomes to form.
Teach us that restraint can build trust
more effectively than arguments fueled by urgency.
Guide us to weigh our responses
so they reflect our values and protect connection.
Let our silence at the right moment
serve as a tool for understanding
rather than avoidance.
Support us as we strive to act
with wisdom that uplifts others.
Shape our relationships
through choices rooted in care,
depth,
and thoughtful direction.
Amen

The silent strength of forebearance shapes long-lasting respect.

~

God,
help us carry a strength that stays steady
even when it remains unseen by others.
Build in us the resolve
to meet conflict with composure
shaped through discipline.
Guide our decisions
so we act with purpose rather than impulse.
Teach us
to let our restraint shape respect
that lasts beyond the moment.
Strengthen our commitment
to creating stability where turmoil once grew.
Let our actions reveal depth
built over time through consistent choices.
Support us in becoming people
whose responses inspire cooperation,
fairness,
and long-term trust.
Lead us into futures
formed through grounded intention.
Amen

KINDNESS

Kindness leaves marks that no eye can see but many hearts can feel.

~

God,
help us offer kindness that shapes hearts
even when it goes unseen by the eye.
Let our actions carry warmth
that settles deeply within those who cross our path.
Teach us to move through the world with a gentleness
that strengthens others without demanding recognition.
Guide our habits so generosity
becomes part of how we live,
speaking through subtle choices
that uplift without fanfare.
Let our kindness travel farther than we imagine,
reaching those who need encouragement
at the right moment.
Shape us into people
who leave others feeling valued,
understood,
and renewed.
Amen

A small act of kindness can redirect the course of someone's day.

~

God,
guide us to offer small gestures
that shift the tone of someone's entire day.
Help us see moments where a word,
a smile,
or a simple act can redirect heaviness into hope.
Teach us to pay attention
to the people around us
so we notice when someone carries more than they show.
Let our kindness work quietly,
restoring strength in ways we may never witness.
Help us give freely,
trusting that even the smallest generosity
becomes part of a larger path
someone is walking.
Shape our intentions
so kindness becomes our instinctive way of living.
Amen

True kindness asks for nothing in return yet gives everything.

~

God,
help us give kindness without
expecting anything in return.
Teach us to share from a place of abundance
rather than seeking reward.
Strengthen our hearts
so our generosity becomes a steady expression of compassion.
Guide us to lift burdens,
speak gently,
and act with sincerity even when no one is watching.
Let our kindness carry healing
where words alone cannot reach.
Help us offer comfort,
encouragement,
and support with no desire for praise.
Shape us into people
who contribute love to the world
simply because it is needed.
Let our giving create futures filled with hope.
Amen

Words seasoned with kindness linger longer than any command.

~

God,
guide our speech so our words carry kindness
that lasts beyond the moment.
Help us choose language that steadies,
strengthens,
and supports those around us.
Teach us to use our voice with care,
adding gentleness to conversations
that might otherwise wound.
Let our words linger as encouragement
rather than spite.
Inspire us to speak in ways that bring calm,
connection,
and healing.
Help us recognize the weight a single sentence can hold.
Let our speech create memories
that comfort long after the moment has passed.
Shape our communication
so it builds rather than harms.
Amen

Kindness grows quietly, spreading where force cannot reach.

~

God,
help kindness grow within us
in ways others may not notice at first.
Teach us that steady goodness reaches places
force never could.
Let our actions spread through simple choices
that open hearts rather than close them.
Guide us to trust the slow growth of love,
knowing it often begins quietly.
Strengthen our desire to help others
without searching for recognition.
Let our lives form gentle pathways
where compassion travels freely.
Help us plant small seeds
that mature into lasting transformation,
touching lives we may never meet.
Shape us into channels of steady,
expanding goodness.
Amen

Offering kindness is a choice to make the world softer.

~

God,
teach us to choose kindness
as a way of softening the world.
Help us bend reality toward gentleness
through our actions,
even when the world seems sharp.
Guide us to respond to stress,
conflict,
and uncertainty with generosity
rather than harshness.
Let our kindness become a steady influence
that shifts environments and hearts.
Strengthen our willingness to help
even when it takes effort.
Let every caring act ripple outward,
lifting spirits and awakening hope.
Shape us into people who bring comfort
where there was strain
and warmth where there was distance.
Amen

Even brief gestures of kindness can spark lasting change.

~

God,
help us remember that brief gestures
can ignite lasting transformation.
Teach us to value the moments that seem small,
for they often carry hidden power.
Guide us to lend a hand,
offer a kind word,
or give encouragement
that becomes someone's turning point.
Let our kindness spark change
that continues long after we have moved on.
Strengthen our awareness
so we recognize how deeply a single act can matter.
Help us show up fully even in quick interactions.
Shape our habits
so kindness radiates naturally
and plants seeds of hope in unexpected places.
Amen

Kindness is a mirror—what you give returns in unexpected ways.

~

God,
help us see kindness
as a reflection of our inner life.
Teach us that what we offer
often returns through surprising paths.
Guide our actions so we choose generosity
not for gain,
but because it aligns with who we seek to become.
Let our kindness ripple outward
and eventually find its way back
in forms we never predicted.
Strengthen us to act with openness,
generosity,
and sincerity.
Help us accept the gifts that return
when we share freely.
Shape us into people whose kindness travels far,
circles back,
and enriches our journey.
Amen

To practice kindness is to invest in unseen futures.

~

God,
teach us that every act of kindness
invests in futures we may never witness.
Guide us to trust that what we give today
builds something meaningful for tomorrow.
Help us offer compassion that creates possibilities
for those who feel limited or overlooked.
Let our generosity open doors in the lives of others.
Strengthen our commitment to doing good
even when the results remain unseen.
Help us become builders of better days
through choices that seem simple
but carry lasting value.
Shape our hearts
to plant hope in places that need new beginnings.
Amen

Kindness can tame the sharp edges of anger and fear.

~

God,
help us let kindness soften anger
and fear wherever they rise.
Teach us to meet tension
with gentleness that lowers walls
and quiets hostility.
Guide us to respond in ways that reduce harm
rather than amplify it.
Strengthen our ability to bring peace
where emotions run high.
Let our kindness show that compassion can transform
even rigid moments.
Help us move through conflict
with careful generosity,
offering a steadying presence
for those who feel overwhelmed.
Shape us into people
who calm storms with empathy and care.
Amen

The strength of kindness lies not in grandeur but in consistency.

~

God,
help us practice kindness consistently,
not only in grand moments
but in the ordinary rhythm of our days.
Teach us that steady compassion
often holds more power
than any dramatic gesture.
Guide our habits so we bring encouragement
into routines that feel repetitive.
Strengthen our willingness
to help when no one expects anything from us.
Let kindness form the backbone of our choices.
Help us offer support,
warmth,
and understanding with regularity.
Shape us into people
whose steady goodness builds trust
and strengthens bonds that last.
Amen

Kindness speaks louder when it meets resistance.

~

God,
guide us to show kindness
even when we face resistance.
Teach us to remain grounded in compassion
when the world pushes back.
Strengthen our courage
so we continue doing good despite difficulty.
Help us understand that kindness
can carry weight when circumstances grow tense.
Let our response become a turning point
that softens hardened hearts.
Support us in keeping our footing
when generosity is met with skepticism.
Shape us into people
whose kindness stands firm,
offering stability where turmoil tries to dominate.
Amen

Acts of kindness often cost nothing yet weigh heavily in memory.

~

God,
help us remember that kindness
often costs nothing yet is remembered for years.
Teach us to give freely from the heart,
offering what lifts others without expecting return.
Guide our actions
so we enrich the memories of those we encounter.
Let our kindness ease burdens
that others carry silently.
Strengthen our awareness
so we recognize chances to help
before they slip away.
Shape our habits
so generosity becomes part of our daily life.
Let our actions form stories that stay with others
long after the moment has passed.
Amen

Kindness can be revolutionary in a world built on haste.

~

God,
help us bring kindness into a world
that often moves too quickly.
Teach us that compassion
can challenge the frantic pace around us.
Guide us to slow down enough
to notice when someone needs a gentle word
or a supportive action.
Strengthen us to stand against coldness
by offering warmth wherever we can.
Let our kindness push back
against haste
and create room for genuine connection.
Help us live in ways that add softness
where the world feels jagged.
Shape us into people
who anchor moments with genuine care.
Amen

Let your kindness be a quiet current that reshapes the tide around you.

~

God,
let our kindness move through the world
like a steady current that subtly
reshapes everything it touches.
Teach us to carry gentleness in our actions
so change forms naturally rather than through force.
Guide our steps so we bring ease
where there was tension
and hope where there was fatigue.
Strengthen us to keep choosing kindness
even when the environment grows challenging.
Let our influence transform spaces quietly,
shifting the atmosphere toward compassion.
Help us cultivate a way of living that guides others
toward goodness without demanding anything.
Amen

GOODNESS

Goodness shines brightest when no one is watching.

~

God,
guide us to act with sincerity
even when no one knows what we have done.
Help us choose what is right
simply because it is right,
not because it earns praise.
Strengthen our commitment to walk with integrity
in the hidden spaces of our lives.
Let our unseen efforts shape who we become,
grounding us in character that lasts.
Teach us to value the inner work
that shapes our outer path.
Help us carry a spirit that honors truth
even in isolation.
Form us into people who shine from within,
regardless of audience or recognition.
Amen

Every choice for goodness is a step toward a stronger world.

~

God,
help us understand
that every choice built on integrity
contributes to a stronger world.
Guide us to act with purpose that uplifts others
and stabilizes our foundations.
Strengthen our will to choose
what benefits the whole
rather than what brings short-term gain.
Let our daily decisions shape communities
marked by fairness,
compassion,
and growth.
Teach us to see that each step taken with sincerity
creates momentum toward a better future.
Support us as we commit to actions that build,
protect,
and inspire.
Form our journey
so it adds strength to the world around us.
Amen

Goodness is built slowly, one intentional act at a time.

~

God,
help us build meaningful lives
through consistent acts rooted in intention.
Teach us to value small choices
that accumulate into lasting impact.
Guide us to act thoughtfully,
knowing that steady commitment
shapes a path worth following.
Strengthen us to focus on what fosters growth,
connection,
and a solid moral foundation.
Let our intentions remain steady
even when progress feels slow.
Help us understand
that meaningful work often grows quietly over time.
Shape our daily actions
so they contribute to a life filled with purpose,
compassion,
and honorable character.
Amen

The weight of goodness is light when carried with sincerity.

~

God,
teach us to carry sincerity in all we do,
making what is good
feel light instead of burdensome.
Guide us to act from the heart
so our choices uplift rather than weigh us down.
Strengthen our spirit so we give without calculation,
offering care freely.
Help us remain genuine
in moments that challenge our consistency.
Let our efforts reflect authenticity,
not performance.
Shape our inner life so goodness
flows naturally and without strain.
Support us
as we learn to live in a way that feels honest,
kind,
and grounded.
Amen

Even small sparks of goodness can ignite larger change.

~

God,
guide us to offer small gestures
that eventually grow into meaningful transformation.
Teach us to trust the influence of simple actions
that touch lives in subtle but lasting ways.
Strengthen our belief
that our efforts matter
even when the results are unseen.
Help us bring warmth into moments others overlook.
Let our kindness spread from one person to another,
widening its reach.
Support us as we choose generosity
in situations that feel minor
yet hold hidden power.
Shape us into people who spark change
through compassion expressed in everyday life.
Amen

Goodness often grows in the spaces between ambition and humility.

~

God,
help us cultivate goodness
in the places where ambition meets humility.
Teach us to stay grounded
even while we pursue meaningful goals.
Guide us so our efforts are shaped by character,
not ego.
Strengthen us to make choices
that lift others rather than overshadow them.
Help us remember that progress is strongest
when supported by sincerity.
Let our journey reflect both drive and compassion,
balancing achievement with care.
Support us as we walk paths
that value humanity
as much as accomplishment.
Form us into people
who lead with heart as well as skill.
Amen

True goodness resists the lure of shortcuts and excuses.

~

God,
guide us to remain steady
when excuses seem tempting
and shortcuts appear easy.
Teach us
to stand firm in what we know is right,
even when it requires effort.
Strengthen our commitment
to follow through with honesty and discipline.
Help us build habits
that reflect our values instead of convenience.
Let our devotion to what is right
shape our choices and define our path.
Support us in moments
when difficulty tries to sway us.
Shape our hearts
so integrity becomes the anchor
of every decision we make.
Amen

Goodness thrives where integrity meets action.

~

God,
help us unite integrity with action
so our beliefs and behaviors remain aligned.
Teach us to live our values
instead of speaking them without follow-through.
Guide us to act with consistency,
ensuring that our commitments
shape our daily steps.
Strengthen our desire
to build trust through reliability and authenticity.
Let our choices reflect a life guided by principle.
Support us as we bring truth into practice,
shaping environments marked
by fairness and compassion.
Form us into people
whose actions speak clearly and honorably.
Amen

Each act of goodness strengthens the unseen threads connecting us.

~

God,
help us strengthen the invisible bonds
that connect us to one another
through every act rooted in goodness.
Teach us that our choices
affect more lives than we realize.
Guide us to lift others in ways
that encourage unity and hope.
Strengthen our awareness
so we recognize how our actions
weave into the fabric of community.
Let every thoughtful gesture
reinforce the ties that keep us standing together.
Support us in building relationships
marked by honesty and care.
Shape us into people
who strengthen the world through genuine connection.
Amen

Goodness leaves a legacy that neither time nor distance can erase.

~

God,
help us contribute to a legacy
that outlasts time,
distance,
and memory.
Teach us to plant seeds
that continue to grow long after we have moved on.
Guide us to act with intention
so our lives leave a trail of compassion for others to follow.
Strengthen our desire
to build something lasting
through kindness and integrity.
Let our influence ripple into future generations.
Support us in making choices
that uplift those who come after us.
Shape our impact so it lives beyond the moment.
Amen

Choosing goodness can calm storms we cannot control.

~

God,
help us bring steadiness into storms
that are beyond our control.
Teach us to offer calm through kindness
and wisdom when chaos surrounds us.
Guide us to bring grounding presence
into situations filled with uncertainty.
Strengthen our ability to help others
find balance when fear rises.
Let our actions introduce peace
where disturbance once ruled.
Support us in becoming a source of strength
for those who need it.
Shape us into people
who anchor turbulent moments with compassion.
Amen

Goodness is subtle; its impact is measured in depth, not volume.

~

God,
teach us to value depth over noise
in our efforts to contribute good to the world.
Guide us to act with substance
rather than seeking attention.
Strengthen our desire
to focus on what truly matters,
not what gains applause.
Help us slip past superficial distractions
and invest in meaningful action.
Let our influence become powerful
through sincerity and consistency.
Support us as we build lives
marked by substance and care.
Shape us
so our contributions reach deeper than the surface.
Amen

The roots of goodness deepen when nourished by understanding.

~

God,
help us deepen our commitment to what is right
through understanding and empathy.
Teach us to listen well
so our actions emerge from insight
rather than assumption.
Guide us to respond with compassion
that grows roots in wisdom.
Strengthen our ability to meet others where they are,
offering support that truly helps.
Let our choices reflect thoughtfulness
shaped through genuine care.
Support us as we build lives
rooted in awareness and fairness.
Shape us into people who nurture goodness
through insight and love.
Amen

Goodness carried consistently becomes a force no barrier can stop.

~

God,
help us carry consistency
in our pursuit of what is right,
forming a force stronger than any barrier.
Teach us to continue doing good
even when obstacles appear.
Guide us to stand firm in character
so our actions grow powerful over time.
Strengthen our endurance
so we remain true to our values.
Let our steady choices carve paths
where change can flourish.
Support us in becoming pillars
that others lean on
when situations grow difficult.
Shape us into people who persevere with integrity.
Amen

Even in complexity, goodness finds a path through.

~

God,
guide us through complicated moments
with a commitment to kindness and fairness.
Teach us that even in tangled circumstances,
a path forward exists
when we remain grounded in what is right.
Strengthen our ability
to stay true to our values
when faced with uncertainty.
Help us act with clarity of purpose
that brings healing instead of harm.
Let our choices illuminate possibilities
where confusion once lived.
Support us as we walk through challenging terrain
with courage and compassion.
Shape us into people
who forge steady paths through complexity.
Amen

FAITHFULNESS

Faithfulness stands steady when circumstances sway.

~

God,
guide us when events shift around our lives.
Strengthen our resolve
so we stand firm in what we promised.
Help us act with steadiness
that does not weaken when pressure rises.
Shape our choices
so they match our values,
even when progress feels slow.
Keep our minds clear
so we do not chase impulses
that pull us from our path.
Teach us to grow
through change
without losing our purpose.
Help us move forward
with steady hearts
and grounded decisions that endure.
Let our character hold strong
through every season.
Amen

True faithfulness is shown in small, repeated acts, not grand gestures.

~

God,
help us honor each day
with simple acts
that strengthen our commitment.
Keep us from seeking dramatic efforts
that distract from the steady work
that truly shapes us.
Build in us a rhythm
that supports real growth.
Let our choices reflect responsibility
more than display.
Remind us that long-term strength forms
through repeated effort
rather than sudden bursts.
Guide our steps
so each small task contributes to meaningful progress.
Give us endurance
to follow through when motivation fades.
Help us value steady practice
as the path to deeper purpose.
Amen

Faithfulness builds trust that no storm can erode.

~

God,
anchor us
so trust grows through how we live,
not through what we claim.
When challenges rise,
help us stand firm without losing focus.
Strengthen our resolve
so setbacks do not break what we are building.
Teach us to carry consistency
into every part of our lives.
Let our actions form a foundation
that cannot be shaken by doubt or strain.
Keep us committed to truth,
fairness,
and responsibility.
Help us remain reliable
when conditions test us.
Let our loyalty and strength
create bonds
that hold through every storm.
Amen

Even unseen, faithfulness shapes the world around it.

~

God,
shape our efforts so they matter
even when no one speaks of them.
Remind us that steady commitment
influences the world in ways we may not see.
Guide our choices
so our work carries lasting value.
Help us remember
that meaningful progress often grows slowly.
Strengthen our resolve
so we keep acting with purpose
even when results remain distant.
Teach us to support others
through consistent action
rather than seeking recognition.
Form in us a heart that stays true
even when circumstances feel uncertain.
Let our character speak through what we do daily.
Amen

To remain faithful is to honor commitments without seeking reward.

~

God,
teach us to honor every promise we make
without seeking reward.
Form in us a commitment
rooted in integrity rather than praise.
Help us follow through
even when the task feels tiring
or inconvenient.
Strengthen our will
so we keep moving forward
with responsibility at the center.
Keep our motives aligned with what is right,
not with what benefits us.
Let us stand firm in purpose
even when no one acknowledges our efforts.
Give us courage to uphold our word
in all conditions.
Amen

Faithfulness is the quiet backbone of lasting connections.

~

God,
strengthen our connections
through consistency and care.
Help us support one another
with actions that hold true over time.
Guide our efforts
so we build relationships
that last beyond changing moods
or shifting conditions.
Help us contribute to a foundation
others can rely on.
Teach us to act with reliability
rather than seeking perfection.
Give us steady hearts
that remain committed
when life becomes demanding.
Let our dedication create bonds
that grow stronger across the years.
Amen

Time tests faithfulness, revealing its depth and resilience.

~

God,
guide us through the seasons
that test our endurance.
Help us stay true
to what we believe
even when time stretches our resolve.
Strengthen our ability to continue
with integrity when challenges rise slowly
instead of suddenly.
Give us a spirit that does not weaken
as demands increase.
Teach us to value the long path
rather than seeking a shortcut.
Help us grow stronger through trials
that require long-lasting commitment.
Let our choices show depth
and stability formed through ongoing work.
Amen

Faithfulness grows when consistency meets integrity.

~

God,
help us join consistency with integrity
so our lives grow in strength.
Let our actions
reflect what we claim to value.
Guide our steps
so reliability becomes natural to us.
Strengthen our resolve
when the easy path tempts us away
from our purpose.
Teach us to follow through even
when the rewards are not immediate.
Help us build character
through daily effort.
Let our choices form patterns
that lead to long-term growth
and honest living.
Amen

A faithful presence often matters more than perfect solutions.

~

God,
give us the strength
to bring care into each situation
without believing we must fix everything.
Help us show support
through steady action
rather than chasing perfect answers.
Guide us so our reliability
brings comfort to those around us.
Teach us to be present
with courage and purpose.
Keep us aware of the needs before us
without becoming overwhelmed by them.
Let our consistency offer stability
where uncertainty tries to grow.
Strengthen our ability to serve with steady hearts.
Amen

Faithfulness turns ordinary efforts into enduring impact.

~

God,
guide us so our everyday efforts
create results that last beyond the moment.
Teach us
that long-term influence
often grows from simple acts
done with genuine commitment.
Help us continue
even when progress feels small.
Strengthen our resolve
so we do not abandon purposeful work
for easier paths.
Keep us focused
on the value of steady practice.
Let our actions form ripples
that expand through time,
shaping more than we expect.
Help us build a life
where consistency becomes strength.
Amen

Where faithfulness lives, doubt loses its power.

~

God,
help us grow strong in faith
so doubt loses its hold on our choices.
Teach us to act with confidence
rooted in steady commitment.
Guide us
so our decisions reflect trust
instead of fear.
Strengthen our resolve
when uncertainty surrounds us.
Let our lives show
what devoted action can achieve.
Keep us focused on truth
and responsibility rather than anxiety.
Help us move forward
with hearts anchored in purpose.
Amen

The strength of faithfulness is proven in moments of temptation.

~

God,
give us strength
when we face moments that tempt us
away from our commitments.
Help us see the real cost of choices
that pull us from what we value.
Strengthen our will
so we stand firm when challenged.
Teach us to stay devoted
even when easier options call to us.
Let us act from integrity rather than impulse.
Guide our steps
so we remain aligned with what is right,
steady,
and true.
Amen

Faithfulness is a choice renewed each day, not a one-time decision.

~

God,
remind us each day
that commitment must be renewed
if it is to live.
Help us bring fresh dedication
to the responsibilities before us.
Strengthen our resolve
so we do not rely on yesterday's efforts
to carry today's challenges.
Teach us to approach our tasks
with renewed purpose.
Let our daily choices
confirm the values we hold.
Guide us
so we remain steady
even when circumstances demand more from us.
Amen

Even in silence, faithfulness speaks volumes.

~

God,
help us speak through how we live
even when words feel limited.
Teach us that steady action communicates
far more than declarations.
Guide us so our choices
reveal genuine commitment.
Strengthen our resolve
so our loyalty becomes clear
through what we do each day.
Help us contribute strength
and stability to those around us.
Give us the courage
to act with consistency
even in difficult seasons.
Amen

Faithfulness is the bridge between intention and fulfillment.

~

God,
guide us
as we step from intention to completion.
Help us build a life
where our actions fulfill
what our hearts plan to do.
Strengthen our discipline
so our efforts reach their full purpose.
Teach us to stay steady
when the path becomes demanding.
Keep our focus sharp
so we do not stop halfway.
Help us bridge the gap between desire
and accomplishment through committed work.
Let our dedication carry us
to the outcomes we seek.
Amen

GENTLENESS

Gentleness can move obstacles that force cannot budge.

~

God,
shape our strength
so it moves obstacles through calm intention
rather than force.
Help us meet resistance
with steady character
that shifts what pressure cannot.
Teach us to carry firmness
without aggression
and purpose without harshness.
Help us approach challenges
with hearts that stay steady
even when circumstances strain us.
Strengthen our ability to move forward
with thoughtful action that creates lasting change.
Let our influence reshape what seems stuck,
not through impact
but through steady direction that opens new paths.
Keep us committed to constructive choices
that move us toward meaningful progress.
Amen

A touch of gentleness often softens hearts harder than stone.

~

God,
help us bring a touch of softness
when others brace for conflict.
Strengthen us
so our presence eases tension
rather than deepening it.
Teach us to respond in ways that reach
where rigidity fails.
Let our words and actions create space for healing
where hardness once stood.
Help us meet difficult people
with grounded character
that stays steady instead of reactive.
Shape us into people
who disarm hostility through steady purpose.
Let our efforts open doors
that pressure alone cannot move.
Fill our interactions with strength
that works beneath the surface.
Amen

True gentleness carries strength beneath its calm surface.

~

God,
teach us to carry strength
that does not need noise
or intensity to be real.
Help us move through challenges
with steadiness anchored beneath our calm choices.
Let our actions speak with weight
even when they appear gentle.
Strengthen our spirit
so we never confuse softness with weakness.
Help us rely on grounded intention
rather than force.
Shape our days
so our influence grows through stability and purpose.
Let our character stand firm
without aggression
and hold steady without domination.
Help us show that real strength
often rests beneath a calm exterior.
Amen

Gentleness is a choice that reshapes every interaction.

~

God,
help us choose actions
that reshape each moment for the better.
Strengthen our ability
to respond with care even when tension rises.
Let our choices turn difficult interactions
into meaningful ones.
Teach us to meet challenges
with thoughtfulness rather than reaction.
Keep us focused on creating connection
instead of conflict.
Help us hold to values
that bring peace into situations
that might otherwise fracture.
Let our actions carry the power
to shift the atmosphere
simply through grounded presence.
Teach us to build each moment
through steady kindness that endures.
Amen

Even in urgency, gentleness preserves dignity.

~

God,
help us act with urgency when required
while still honoring the worth of others.
Strengthen us
so our decisions never strip dignity
from those involved.
Teach us to move efficiently
without losing compassion.
Help us act with steadiness
even when time presses in.
Let our choices uplift rather than diminish.
Keep our hearts anchored
so that speed never leads to harm.
Help us handle pressure with character strong enough
to remain caring under strain.
Let our actions show that efficiency
and kindness can work together without conflict.
Amen

Gentleness lingers where harshness fades.

~

God,
help us bring actions
that remain long after harsh words fade.
Strengthen us
so we leave a positive mark
that lasts beyond the moment.
Teach us to act with purpose
that reaches others deeply.
Let our efforts carry weight
not through force but through sincerity.
Help us build connections
that endure through consistency.
Keep our choices aligned with kindness
that grows stronger over time.
Let our presence bring steadiness
that supports those who need it.
Teach us to create influence
that remains long
after the noise of conflict disappears.
Amen

Acts of gentleness ripple far beyond their origin.

~

God,
help us send out actions
that reach farther than we expect.
Strengthen us so our choices create effects
that continue long after we take them.
Teach us to act thoughtfully,
knowing small efforts can shape
more than we imagine.
Let our kindness ripple into places
we may never see.
Help us build a world
where steady actions
create momentum toward good.
Keep our intentions steady
so what begins with us
grows into something lasting.
Let our contributions
travel through the lives of others
with meaningful impact.
Amen

Gentleness can guide without commanding.

~

God,
help us move through life
without controlling others.
Strengthen us
so our actions influence through steadiness
rather than command.
Teach us to inspire rather than impose.
Let our choices encourage cooperation
instead of pressure.
Help us carry a presence
that leads others toward peace without force.
Keep us grounded
so we never rely on domination to create progress.
Let our actions show that strength
can create movement without demands.
Teach us to build environments
where people feel supported to act with integrity.
Amen

The power of gentleness lies in its subtle persistence.

~

God,
help us stay steady with determination
that endures through time.
Strengthen us so our efforts continue
even when progress seems slow.
Teach us to act with consistency
that wears down resistance
without aggression.
Let our dedication carry the force
to shape outcomes in lasting ways.
Keep us anchored
to what matters
so we do not abandon important work.
Help us stay engaged
even when challenges stretch longer than expected.
Let our persistence remain strong
through every season.
Amen

Gentleness tempers words, turning them into bridges instead of walls.

~

God,
help us form words that heal instead of divide.
Strengthen our ability to speak with care
when tension rises.
Teach us to shape communication
that builds connection rather than barriers.
Let our sentences carry weight without harm.
Keep us aware
of how speech can strengthen relationships
when offered with intention.
Help us choose language
that supports understanding
rather than conflict.
Let our conversations open paths
toward cooperation
instead of shutting them down.
Amen

In gentleness, patience and understanding meet.

~

God,
help us blend understanding
with calm steadiness
in every moment.
Strengthen us
so our choices reflect compassion
joined with clarity of thought.
Teach us to handle challenges
with an approach that brings people together.
Let our actions show that strength
and kindness work seamlessly.
Keep us committed to decisions
that reflect fairness and care.
Help us stay centered
so confusion does not sway us from what is right.
Let our lives show the power of balanced character.
Amen

Gentleness is strength wrapped in kindness.

~

God,
help us hold strength wrapped in kindness
that reaches others with depth.
Strengthen us
so we respond with grace even when tension rises.
Teach us to carry influence
without aggression.
Let our actions show that caring choices
carry real power.
Keep our hearts steady
so we do not mirror hostility
when confronted with it.
Help us show that kindness
can achieve what pressure cannot.
Let our lives reflect a type of strength
that uplifts rather than harms.
Amen

Small gestures of gentleness often carry the deepest impact.

~

God,
help us bring small gestures
that touch others deeply.
Strengthen us
so we never underestimate
the impact of a simple act.
Teach us to notice the moments
where we can bring comfort,
support,
or encouragement.
Let our kindness reach those who feel unseen
or overwhelmed.
Keep our choices centered on
what brings connection.
Help us build a pattern of meaningful actions
that shape lives in lasting ways.
Let each small effort become part
of a larger work of compassion.
Amen

Choosing gentleness transforms conflict into connection.

~

God,
help us choose responses
that turn tension into connection.
Strengthen us so we remain calm
when conflict presses in.
Teach us to act with intention
that opens doors rather than closing them.
Let our presence transform strained interactions
into opportunities for understanding.
Keep us from reacting in ways
that deepen division.
Help us bring steadiness that encourages unity.
Let our actions create pathways
toward healing where separation once grew.
Amen

Gentleness is a steady force, quiet yet undeniable.

~

God,
help us move through each day
with a strength that does not depend
on volume or force.
Strengthen us so our steady choices
create meaningful change.
Teach us to act with consistency
that accumulates impact over time.
Let our influence shape lives
through substance rather than intensity.
Keep us centered
so challenges do not break our focus.
Help us bring a presence
that shifts situations
through unwavering character.
Let our strength show through actions that endure.
Amen

SELF CONTROL

Self-control turns impulse into deliberate action.

~

God,
empower us to turn quick impulses
into deliberate action.
When urges surge,
grant us the inner space to choose with purpose.
Let our decisions rise from intention
shaped by who we seek to become,
not the demand of the moment.
Teach us to act from thoughtful conviction
so our days form a life directed by meaning.
As emotions shift,
keep our inner landscape balanced
and ready for wise response.
May our choices today
build a future anchored in discipline
practiced across time.
Amen

True power is often measured by our level of restraint.

~

God,
remind us that real power
appears in restraint.
When pressure pushes us toward forceful reactions,
let a measured spirit guide our next step.
Grant us the confidence to trust calmer choices,
knowing they build far more
than intensity ever could.
Let our minds settle enough
to think clearly before acting.
May our responses carry intention
shaped through practice.
When challenges rise,
keep our vision set on actions
that develop our character beyond the moment.
Amen

Self-control is the slow steady victory over fleeting desire.

~

God,
grant us the ability to meet fleeting desire
with thoughtful discipline.
When cravings flash,
allow our intentions to govern the moment.
Keep our minds centered
on long-term purpose
instead of temporary pull.
Let our commitments remain firm
even when emotion tries to sway us.
May each deliberate choice form a pattern
that strengthens our inner framework.
Let our lives be shaped by direction
rooted in meaningful pursuit,
not impulse.
Amen

Mastery begins when choice outweighs reaction.

~

God,
grant us the power
to choose action over reaction.
When emotion strikes,
create a pause within us
where purpose can rise.
Let our decisions reflect intention
instead of old habits.
When conflict appears,
allow us to move from principle
and not instinct.
Form responses in us
that build progress and not chaos.
May every interaction
reveal a commitment
to mature decision-making.
Amen

Self-control shapes character more than circumstance ever can.

~

God,
let our character take the lead
when circumstances change.
When situations grow unpredictable,
keep our values at the center of our choices.
Allow our inner standards
to speak louder than external pressure.
May our repeated decisions
form a foundation
that outlasts changing conditions.
Let each moment
sharpen the person we are becoming,
and let our actions
reflect integrity shaped over time.
Amen

The strongest decisions are tempered by self-control.

~

God,
grant us choices
tempered by self-control.
When intensity rises,
let intentional thought hold the moment
long enough for wisdom to form.
Allow our direction
to emerge from discipline
built through consistency.
May our daily actions
reflect the deeper purpose we carry within.
Let our lives move through decisions
crafted with care in both calm and tension.
Amen

Self-control creates space where clarity can grow.

~

God,
open space within us
where insight can grow.
When emotion pushes,
allow an inner pause to settle over us
so purpose can surface.
Let restraint
create room for understanding.
May our choices
reflect long-term vision
instead of immediate desire.
Teach us to listen inwardly
before moving outward,
building a life
shaped by thoughtful action.
Amen

Each act of restraint strengthens the mind's resilience.

~

God,
let each small act of restraint
strengthen our resilience.
When impulses rise,
allow us to choose actions
aligned with our deeper aims.
May we appreciate
how minor decisions accumulate
into lasting transformation.
Let our discipline form a path
that continually pulls us toward growth.
May each moment add structure
to the life we are building.
Amen

Self-control allows intention to guide the moment, not habit.

~

God,
allow intention to steer us instead of habit.
When old reactions try to take control,
give us the pause required
for choice to emerge.
Let each moment be a chance
to exercise self-control
that shapes our future.
May our responses reflect commitment
to values formed through practice.
Let our decisions bring order
where emotion once ruled.
Amen

Discipline and self-control are allies, not enemies.

~

God,
unite discipline and self-control
within us
as partners in our progress.
Let their combined influence
guide our path with purpose.
When temptation rises,
allow our chosen direction to remain firm.
May our actions
reflect long-term goals
shaped by consistent practice.
Let our lives
show the freedom that comes from inner order.
Amen

Even small measures of self-control compound into lasting impact.

~

God,
let the small choices
carry great weight within us.
May each moment of restraint
expand our capacity
to face challenges with intention.
When urges press hard,
allow our inner commitments to stand firm.
Let our decisions look beyond
the moment toward the unfolding future.
May every act
contribute to lasting change
shaped by disciplined living.
Amen

Self-control is the foundation of freedom, not restriction.

~

God,
remind us that self-control
expands our freedom.
Let each deliberate choice
free us from impulses
that limit our potential.
When distractions call for our attention,
allow our deeper purpose
to shape the moment.
May our daily decisions
support the life we aim to build.
Let our actions reflect conviction shaped over time.
Amen

When patience meets self-control, progress becomes inevitable.

~

God,
when progress moves slowly,
allow discipline to carry us forward.
Let self-control anchor our actions,
keeping us aligned with long-term intention.
When challenges extend across time,
may we remain committed
to deliberate choices
that build real growth.
Let each moment
reveal our capacity
to rise above fleeting desire.
Amen

Self-control is the calm in the storm of impulse.

~

God,
keep us centered
when impulses swirl around us.
When life pushes toward fast reactions,
grant us the pause required to reclaim choice.
Let intention shape the moment
so chaos loses its pull.
May our decisions reflect the future we aim to build,
not the demands of sudden emotion.
Allow us to move with purpose
even when the atmosphere around us feels tense.
Let our inner direction
remain consistent as we navigate each challenge.
May our actions create harmony
where conflict once grew,
turning each moment into an opportunity
for growth and connection.
Amen

Choosing wisely is the echo of practiced self-control.

~

God,
empower us to choose well in every situation.
Let our decisions rise
from practiced self-control
that shapes our path with intention.
When impulses rush through us,
grant space for thoughtful action to emerge.
May our lives reflect choices anchored
in long-term purpose instead of instant desire.
Allow our discipline to craft patterns
that carry us toward fulfillment.
Let each moment
become a step toward a life
grounded in deliberate action
and meaningful direction.
May our daily practices
form the echo of wisdom we cultivate within.
Amen

Author's Note

Writing this book has been an act of both surrender and discovery. I didn't want to offer polished language or distant spiritual ideals. I wanted to offer honesty, compassion, and prayers that reflect real human experience.

I believe deeply in the way God restores the mind through gentle guidance of character. Every prayer in this book was written with the intention of creating space: space to breathe, space to reflect, space to reconnect with yourself and with God.

If these words bring comfort, clarity, or even a moment of strength and inspiration, then this book has fulfilled its purpose. Thank you for opening these pages and allowing me to share this journey with you.

I pray that something here touched your spirit, steadied your thoughts, or softened the spaces within you that felt tense or overshadowed.

Mental renewal is a lifelong journey, one shaped by grace, patience, and the gentle work of God. Whenever your mind grows weary again (and it will), remember that renewal is always available. Return to these prayers whenever you need grounding, encouragement, or a quiet moment with God.

May peace accompany your decisions.
May clarity shape your days.
May resilience rise quietly within you.
May God continue to restore your mind,
one breath, one prayer, one step at a time.
May these prayers become part of your healing rhythm.

Did you love *Prayers for Mental Renewal*? Then you should read *365 Morning Prayers*[1] by H.B Sky!

[2]

365 Morning Prayers is a beautifully structured full year devotional; designed to nurture spiritual growth, emotional renewal, and inner peace.

The tone is meditative, lyrical, and steady. The prayers balance poetic rhythm with sincerity, focusing on gratitude, faith, resilience, creativity, peace, and divine purpose.

Each day's prayer stands alone yet threads into a larger spiritual journey through the months, from January's renewal and February's faith to March's peace and April's guidance, building a sense of progression from awakening and trust to alignment and service.

---

1. https://books2read.com/u/4EXrWO
2. https://books2read.com/u/4EXrWO

This isn't rigidly doctrinal, it's spiritually rich yet emotionally inclusive. Readers of faith, as well as those drawn to daily mindfulness rooted in divine connection, will find warmth and rhythm in these pages.

365 Morning Prayers is more than a book. It's a spiritual calendar for intentional living.

A perfect Christmas or New Year's Day gift, it offers a year of reflection, calm, and purpose through daily conversation with God.

Also by H.B Sky

A word a Day

A Word a Day Old Testament

Miracle Prayers

Prayers for Health and Healing

Oh Lord Guide Me Prayers for Clarity and Direction

The Lord Shall Supply all my Needs

Standalone

Love, Kisses and Prayers

When Christ Affirms Me

365 Morning Prayers

My Little Book of Affirmations

Prayers for Mental Renewal

www.ingramcontent.com/pod-product-compliance
Lightning Source LLC
LaVergne TN
LVHW090408210926
848480LV00002B/502